SAD GRAVE OF AN IMPERIAL MONGOOSE

SAD GRAVE
of an
IMPERIAL
MONGOOSE

Geoffrey Grigson

MACMILLAN

SBN 333 14084 2

First published 1973 by
MACMILLAN LONDON LIMITED
London and Basingstoke
Associated companies in New York Dublin
Melbourne Johannesburg and Madras

Printed in Great Britain by
A. WHEATON AND CO.
Exeter

for H.M.J.G.

He faces either way,
Yet his month may know a pleasant day.
Whom but the giver
Should the sweetly given pay?

CONTENTS

THE CHAPEL

This being one of the days for me
When the word death tolls, I find
The chapel of O Spes Unica
I've driven to see is closed;

In which, on black touch, a poet
Of a poet says "I was his friend."
For whatever reason, because a boy
Yesterday smashed off a staid

Effigy's alabaster toes, or because
Today the verger's dead or to his
Married daughter in Nottingham goes, I say
The chapel of O Spes Unica is closed.

THE OCULI

I said, Your boat is animal,
These are his eyes, he finds a way
With them.

No, you said, the Goddess
Of Launching—if we pray—
Is in the prow. These are her eyes, then:
She comes, she sees, in a swart night,
Down, up, over, again down
Exceptional waves,
With her two eyes—if our prayer-mind is right—
Lent from her head. For our boat, she only
Sees, and we then are comforted.

I said, I have no goddess, no god either,
Inside my head. You said, It's practical,
And shook your head.

These blank lime-whitish
Eyes, defined by lines of black,
Upon the yellow and the red.

NO SPRINKLING OF BRIGHT WEEDS

Earth—that old-hat phrase of superseded days—
goes red with my slack-satin flowers,
my poppies; my cornflowers of absolute blue—
both mix into my wheat. Also out of the ears

with which it's level stares each sepal-criss-
crossed flat corncockle eye,
magenta, without a blink the whole
day into the hot sky.

   Lady, not now. Lady in whose gay
bleached hair with ears of wheat with poppies if not cornflowers and cockles mixed, and in your south love-
in-the-mist and black-pupilled scarlet pheasant's eye,

Sunburned Ceres, you must understand (you catch my
tone) that now across all plains—no longer fields—
your very carefully treated wheat must be
a clean stand for maximated yields.

Our bodily, of course our economic and our
advertising needs
permit, Lady, except among peasants backward on thin soil,
no sprinkling of bright weeds.

HILL OF THE BEES

Under terracettes and bushes of steep slopes
are these: tracks, hollows, holes, maples, yews, most
muscular ash boles. Over streams are:
dips, slades, slacks,
ditches, mint nooks, hunt gates, springs, night.
Into these by old habit
and tenure we do project ourselves or portions
of us or what in degrees of our likeness we inherit.

At least we did; breathe then
they did back again: the whole companionage,
night, springs, hunt gates, mint nooks, slacks, slades,
ditches, dips, streams;
those muscular ash boles, yews, maples, holes, hollows,
tracks, bushes, terracettes, high slopes:
the lot—all that companionage.

That substantial instability, let it
wither and dry, let it—when, say,
night away from a too
great staring of night-killing light at least
in our words "seems breathing"—die,
or be unfelt, we die.
Unpicking the nest of most warm
feathers we have so long, soft if deluding,
from our own breasts, our own undercoverts torn.

PAWLONIA

Undulations of our lake accept,
you might say without surprise,
pawlonia flowers of startling blue,

such to our eyes up a great vegetable-
tree, both high and wide, and on this lake
such altogether startling

capturing blue,
such blue surprise.

Facile the rhymes to blue—
it's much the same if I declare
this doubled blue to you and me

comes altogether new, down from our north
and to each other new—if for your sake
or for our doubled sake

quickly I make this record of tree-
flowers of blue upon, and then above this
regularly slightly undulating lake.

A MYTH ENACTED

They form, these hill-holding uneven elms and limes,
A Hercules in great trouble, for our troubling times,
Lashed down by dwarfs, not resting at ease,
Unable at all, heave, thresh, as he may in a great September
    wind,
To snap the dwarfs' fruit-net of fine strings.
Wind drops, his efforts cease, he has no strength,
Arrows of rain pelt on his prostrate length,
Great Dorset Hercules being no longer lifting thighs and
    knees
Has again collapsed to a soughing moaning rough run of
    trees.

APRÈS LA CHASSE

In Memory of Maurice Beaubrun

Repent. Why? Not a kingdom of
heaven is at hand
where a for once clement king,
viz. otherwise a colonel, absolute,
will check, perhaps, if you do,
if you trust his promises,
his electric torturer's clean hand.

Repent. Yes, enough. But not
because you fear a punishment, or
being shut out. Too late for that.
Repent? Admit at least in pursuit
you went often too far.
Also, in the fair-ground in the distorting
true mirror hesitated to recognize

Sufficiently what you are,
who are not genius or saint also.
Repent, but not too much,
no grub by grub crawling in white. Old
friend, the kingdom, soviet, democracy—no,
the small mild hamlet of free
felicity, brief, is not of such.

7

MORNING

A certain peace comes on a morning
prospective of idleness from hearing
from a hollow, early, cackling
regular, irregular, without precision
of interval or being
hard like noises of machines.
The morning.

Then evening, after anxiousness,
cool, not too numerous insects whose
predation (they too have fertile eggs to lay
and that needs blood) centres
on bared arms and ankles. Our bearded brown
guest from Jamaica, from Van Dyck's
long painting,

A most peaceful character, about
the too regular beat of the wind-pump
brought by an east wind fitfully, says
he thought at first it was a hot
dog thirstily lapping. A dog machine.
It was, and I preferred
the morning.

Tennyson's very aged grandson
(I like two syllables in aged, "My
agèd Uncle Barley") recalls walking
in the eighties, how wonderfully full of peace
were towns and villages, for the railroads had
taken rumbling off the roads, and he preferred
that morning.

SLOW BELL FROM THE HIGH HILL

Childhood is over, all things end,
I no longer half hear my child with children
Playing below me in the half darkness
Of the hollow foreign lane
Where the dead tramp lay.

All things end—if even at first
Growing is an end: all things begin.
Of course, of course. But ends begin,
And with a never out of fashion
Slow bell from the high hill.

NO REPLY TO A QUESTION
HARDLY FAIR

How did the Welsh think of Olwen with
Cheeks like the foxglove
And of the white clover which grew
Where she printed the grass?

And of the slicing off of her giant da's
Head on his muck-heap,
His own muck-heap
At the back of his caer or his rathe?

I look hard at the grumpy suspicious
Curled grub of a Welsh-enclosed
Scholar, who hates the English,
And living; and ask.

MODELS OF DEITY

Goddess of gold-streaked
hair and sweetest navel, naked,
how by white doves killed and slit
throats of kids
and bloodied fleeces
in—above blue sea—high places
aromatic,
could you have been
delighted, and placated?

Your question, late questioner,
is elementary,
and evasive. At least
in my time I was better
than most earlier—
and some later—
models of beastly deity
which you created.

ANDRÉ BAUCHANT'S MILL
UNDER A BRIGHT PINK ROSE

It happens I know who in this abandoned tan-mill
Lived, suffered, and knew being's exquisite delight,
Treading the causey over his loosestrife meadows,
Treading this black, plank bridge which crosses this black river,

To these hollow rooms, this great bread oven now damp
And always cold, this chimney by reversed irons braced;
To this black lane going up through woods of ash.
His mad wife screamed, and silver—all the more—this flat

Valley seemed, silver the nude ash stems, pure the procession
Of small clouds; Roman chariots he imagined in these meadows,
Dancers in evening. Heavy with much grief his now abandoned
Hollow home, and with much loveliness, and leaving it

Down the firm straight raised lane in evening August light,
At the far end of which for me a figure waits, back
I look at the round rose of a startling cloud over his woods
Which are a long grave bar of green, or black, above his home.

ESTABLISHMENT OF SCENTS

i

Her neck.

ii

Broken pink mushrooms.

iii

Pigs.

iv

In wind off the Sound
Not eradicable salt-dampness-and-tar
Of loops of black nets.

v

Sick almond of white
Of erect laurel flowers over
Glitter of compartmented leaves.

vi

And lemon-verbena first caught
And transferred from leaves which catch.

vii

Iron hisses in black water
In the black shop
Of iron dust and blue wasted flakes.

viii

Sniffed out of
Red, orange cardboard cartridge cases,
Warm, spent, in the yaffle valley.

ix

Dead trout revealed:
Male fern dried to their red spots
And the fine saw of their teeth.

x

Dung scented
Dry Indian elephant in frost.

xi

New World,
Down town the subway push of a visible
Thousand bruegel bodies, sour.

xii

Dried piss: recollections-
Of-acts pee'd out in the hot lane
Outside the Sardinian whorehole.

xiii

By Buttermere in wet
The total high honeysuckle
Of an (alder) tree.

xiv

And Colmar lime trees—
No, I propagate no harmony or contrast—
Near the ulcerated Christ.

CAREER OF A SHARP-PROFILED PUBLIC SERVANT

He tied himself to four umbrellas
and jumped—admittedly it was not high—
from the E.E. tower of his father's church.

He rolled, feet together, hands tight to each side,
over primroses to the edge of the cliff on his father's glebe
and stopped—exactly—3 inches from

a fall of 200 feet. He was imprisoned
in the Russian Revolution, and came home
and to test that nerve

climbed to the top of the steel-framed
mile-measurer above that cliff, and stood there
as before, on one foot, in the high wind,

and he became, the manes of our house-master
will learn with relief, the most conventional
pimp of the Crown,

and was ennobled.

FULKE THE BLACK

He lay in bed on holiday, a short grey man
Eyeing the blood-red roses on the ceiling paper,
Imagining he owned six donjons, a Fulke Nera
Who sent missives saying "Hang the bearer,"
A sweaty-bellied, hairy-penis'd,
Heartily laughing raper;
To whom there came *thé Éléphant*, two *brioches*,
And the morning paper.

St.-Hilaire-de-Harcouet

17

THE JUST INHERITANCE

Yes, but I like it, on White Island on sea-
Campion leaning over the Atlantic staring
To water and air meeting. Why not?
Who is the worse because I like it?
Should it be the occasion of a sneer,
From me, or Alvarez, or recent history?
Very well, I hear too the black cow of the ocean
On her weed-rock moaning; if also
Some relief inherited I value.

SAD GRAVE OF AN IMPERIAL MONGOOSE

Under this weeping ash or umbrella tree
protrudes among white and purple crocuses
the small tombstone of a mongoose
inscribed "Darling Riki-tiki. R.I.P."

He died because, when brought 'home'
by a senior member of the Indian Civil Service
on his retirement he could not stand of course the cold
climate of this green vale. And now the Raj having gone,

the Civil Servant having gone (at one of the two universities
of the time he began with a first class degree in the
classical learning, largely, of a former empire), his children too
having gone (he—and they—were cremated and scattered, but he has

an entry in *Who was Who*), the house as well having changed hands
into other families, this stone among broken crocuses over the small
ribs of Riki-tiki pierced a few inches down by threads from
crocus corms and wandering rootlets of the umbrella tree

remains—other than the entry in *Who was Who* and a short piece
imprisoned flatly in a huge back volume of *The Times*—the sole
indication of the career of one who said
"Many of my best friends are Indians", also "Habeas Corpus hardly

could apply to Indians"; as he administered justice
Socratic and Ciceronian under the aegis—a phrase
whose broad propriety he would have
understood—of after all,

an uninspiriting empire. Though it is easy to look back.

19

JOHN HUNTER'S CANAL

Then as requested turning
round my leg, I caught
a particular name
in what the surgeon—

To his pair of student
doctors—said: it was
attached to some canal
by which the blood inside me

From my stitched thigh
fell: canal of that
grand Orion
of the rational

Sky, grand Hunter of out-
rageously extended bones
and bottled twins
and kidney stones

Who paid
Chardin for canvases
of the quiet grace
of man; and also set,

In London, Haydn
in his old age
humming out his *Twelfth
Night* canzonet.

* * *

It was a pleasure—
though there followed
an injected stinging
of some 5 c.c.—

To think this morning
of that bright Orion
of the human calling,
lover of cool

Harmony, injector
of himself—to see—with organisms
of V.D.,
commemorated, not below

Some periwig or Tory
briber's marble, but
—it flattered me—
inside my own anatomy.

POEM OF A. M.

(With a thought for Hercules Seghers)

One light in this black, or bleak, of the world;
The other lights are out:

In this black of the tufted world,
Under the grey opaque,
A single light. I see

One light. It is the first a.m., when other
Lights are out.

VIEW BY MORANDI ON A
BEDROOM STOOL

A small city illuminated shadowed stands
Upon this stool: Italian city on a hill:
Bottles, containers, towers, red,
Reddened by the last or late sunlight.
Boxes are (shadowed) blue, buff amphitheatre
Of a powder puff.
               Stare: swifts scream, a small and old
Italian city at sunset stands upon this stool.
I put it the other way, this hill, this old
Small Italian city of sun-red-looped
Towers, on this hill.

            Swifts scream. Stare:
These coloured objects, for washing and the like,
Upon this stool.

23

ANCIENT VERSES (A FRAGMENT),
SAN PETRONIO, BOLOGNA

Up there, up there, on fire in the pale blue
Sunset ruffled by the wind, the red towers
Behind high palaces watched the evening's
Grand feats of soulfulness . . .

The towers talked softly, then kept quiet: they raised
Their eyes, they tried to follow through the air the secret
Track of those broken words the wind in its turn
Spoke from a lonely eagerness.

(From the Italian of Dino Campana)

OCCASIONS OF BONES

You put a small hand into the chest-tomb,
White chervil around, and found as if
They were a child's bricks wedged or large
Snails, together, unwoken, for winter glued,
Skulls. With skulls was the stone box crammed.

Well, you said, this is the country, different
From England, where living is only a stomping
Pause before being dead. Then our driver
Half round a hard hairpin stopped, grinned
And softly he said it was the point where in the crossness
He'd shot a Tan dead.

We rowed through a blue bay next day,
Skellig held a coif, blue mountains rose,
On a small island we came to land, where
Remnants of a chapel sprawled, the dead
Lay there in scraps as well, washed out
Surprisingly on to the sand. Did then

These white thin ribs and shins
Make us, more than that shock-headed, soon dead
Sallow poet of Ireland, think particularly
—I think not, dead one—on that occasion
Of the sinfulness
Of our own merry sins?

OBSERVATION IN NOVEMBER

In let's say a hundred years when you
Read this about a thing which I to-day
Observed, you'll need, having
Perfected ways of not con-
ceiving or inseeding which are better—
To look in O.E.D. (it's not
In every set of poesy) to find
The meaning of the compound word
We have for it—French Letter.

Hung on barbed wire I saw this
Pallid thing, not long since used,
Walking this Sunday at the cold
End of November. And I would say
This letter—or, God's grief,
This thing embarrassed sex instructors
Name a "sheathe"—
Had no later than last night enclosed
A good-sized, hot, impatient
Member; in turn enclosed, for pleasure
By that cavity (I thought of Villon's
Sagging armouress) which lines
The satin nest. Good-sized—and young—
Again I guess about that member:
At least, the pallid teat
Was more than filled, that pale
Teat—
          Don't cosmically
Sentimentalize
You urge, about pale human seed

Upon a rusted spike at this
Cold end of November.
                    I won't.
I won't go on long-
windedly, but yet shall say, although
Symbolic juxtaposings aren't
In fashion, that
Red berries of three gay kinds
Hung round that swaying letter
Weighted with seed, which I, having
Worn such jackets in my day
For mutual pleasure, and since I am
No priest, shall not condemn as
Filthy wastage by the two-backed
Beast.

            But then, I must report,
From higher trees suspended, en-
filading berries, wire and letter,
My cold eye took in a vegetable
Flow of grey, all curled and grey,
The shade exactly of my head
And of this last cold overcast
November day.
    It was that plant we know
As Old Man's Beard. I stared at it.
And then the words I said were
Merde! and *Shit*! and with
Appropriate feeling *Con de
Con*! I did not stay in that
Grey lane a moment longer, I kicked
A still dry turd away, then walked
Home, carrying an earth-star
And a green ox-bone.

27

COINCIDENCE IN A SUMMER

Near Badminton I hear a quail
which sibilates from late hay
where castellated chimneys smoke,
a peculiar conjunction for a day.

A train passes underground,
the theatrical chimneys smoke away,
the rare quail in conjoined marking of to-day
reiterates its *wet lips* in the hay.

DEVIL OF A STARLING

Above a sagged roof, how ominous,
Solid, intent, patient, waiting
In straight unleaved branches on a day of most
Miserable colourless cold,
Is a sharp starling, black, not even
A jackdaw, raven, or a crow.

Attributing to it a glint in its small eyes
From Mantegna's Garden of Olives or John Milton's Eden,
Glancingly I think, mightn't it after all be Satan,
Less than cormorant size,
Obscenely bold,
Waiting, watching through
A window warm lusts of the young,
Watching through a window, waiting, waiting,
The simultaneous last
Agonies of one
Who is white and old?

LANGUAGE OF STAIRS

Language of stairs: I lie in bed,
You open letters, then you tap,
Tap up quick
On the hollow stairs:
It's something good,
Someone—but who?—
Is coming, or,
A cheque's arrived

(In honesty should I
Reverse these two?),
A book, for once
A not intolerable review.
The speed, lightness
Of taps I interpret knowing
By this stair-language when for us it's
Something pleasurably new.

If it is something else you learn
From opening letters,
You do not
Speak a hollow slow march
Up the stairs, or (I think) give
Way to tears. You go to typing, or the loo,
Having spread the letter by my plate,
For once glad I get up late.

SPLEEN AGAIN OF THE NIGHT
PICNIC

Now in violet the big round moon,
While soup is heated on the track
And blackberries
Fall into our hands:
Sunset-shining
Were the first we picked, the moon
An intimation only in the haze.

Now, in violet this big moon;
Now, stubble glinting; westward, Mars;
Now metal of our picnic table, not
This night air, cold.

They say,
They say, It is serene. But I am not a
Brother of Basho, senriu, not
Haiku, is my kind. I'm
Failed by the abstruse. I say,
It is a full moon rising
In a matt of violet only.
It is stubble only
Because of moonlight glinting, and only
Mars between
The sunset and the risen moon.

And under, somewhere, this great
Space wild cars klaxon
For the wed; and with a trail
A high plane

Underwrites the moon.
And I decay, and my illusions
Go. Grace, which is
Best, is not substantial,
Does not go on, is, against the cruel,
Not strong, recoils
From suffering.

Killing abhorred, the Panchen Lama
Hired Dark and Years to kill
At last the man, in a wet
Dungeon, whom
He could not kill.

OR PERHAPS THE MYSTIC ROSE
BETWEEN THE LEGS

When out at night
I wish to express my wonder
Seeing a whole moon through white
Clouds in a great ring of amber

Past high leaves shining
Of a scented poplar,
God, I say My God,
What a bloody wonder.

I don't claim God in that exclaiming
Has atavistic merit:
It is a shell of a word
I happen to inherit.

Clumsily to that riding orb should
I exclaim "All Men Who've Been"?
Well, if I take to bits My God,
It is that I mean.

SAINTS

Saints, I wish you well,—
Wish interceding you existed in a heaven,
Not—but then exist you don't—not even
In a nothingness termed (correctly?) hell.

Walking along I see niches
Emptied of fantasies of you, on churches
Where shrines broken shrined
Most wonder-working bits

Of you. Saints, between us, let us be agreed,
Whether you are or not, or were, that I a misery
Still through thinking of you with miseries
Of my black being intercede.

WHITE TOM'S POSITION

Tom, Tom, the pedants' father,
Master of perhaps and rather.

Join your fingers, cross your knees,
Tell young poets to say please.

From your perch in Russell Square
Teach duchesses the art of prayer.

Teach the Tories to discount
Your master's Sermon on the Mount.

Teach the flaccid is the sound,
Proclaim the Pegasus of Pound.

Gird at Lawrence, Hardy, Blake,
For the Church of England's sake—

    etc., and soon

      Over the Missouri, over the Seine,
        Over the Thames, and over the Severn,
      The soul of white Tom
        Shall float to Heaven.

NOTE FOR A GENEALOGICAL TREE

My father dying well past eighty
Spoke almost in coma of a girl
He loved when he was twenty.

Theology was his reading then.
"I say nothing of my reading," so his student's
Diary went, "it was theology,"

And he was soon ordained, and so (I think)
His wilder being mostly
Was contained.

Her home was Ventnor, things
About this girl from Ventnor (he sent
Her roses) from his diary he erased.

My mother—what did she dream of, young?
Old, in her drawing-room, filling her armchair,
By a February fire,

She slept. Her last son's young
Wife sighed, she heard, she snapped
"Ridiculous!" and slept.

PADDINGTON STREET

By the low gas fire which sent
Its red suffusion through the room
I undressed you; to your sweet
Navel bare, and small, exquisitely
Shaped you were.
Yet in that dry warm unharsh gloom
You reached over (horizontally)
And took the phone. You rang
Your husband, and you said,
I shall not be home. And, I am not alone.
I loved you. But what hating
Made you, over me, your breast
Touching my own, most graceful
One, reach to the phone?

GALINGALE

From the living I have been lately in hiding,
in refuge in a verbal past,
how galingale for instance anciently
from the Chinese came, the gingery
rhizome out of Kao-liang.

This antiquarianism will not last,
that sharp ferret Again of sentiment or of pain
will make me bolt; I don't exactly wait, a stone,
a panicle, a tone, a word
out of a mouth alive, glittering, again.

A DOZEN FACTS OF LONDON

Innumerable bodies in clothes mell along the veins of our city. Here are joints, in a side-vein, where money is paid to see bodies removing clothes, and then not shaking invisible quims. This cannot be transferred to beetles. Cats do not understand. Micro-organisms are too busy spreading as always into tracts for living. The booted Black Guards and the Pigs off duty keep to their seats, not even handling their tucked away cocks. The play proceeds.

I have been on the beaches of the filthy Thames, and have found a brown domino, a three and a two, of mutton bone, stuck in grey slime between the pebbles.

A bald crone sells smoked fish in Brewer Street. It might be the phloem of a soft tree she slices from the back of a sturgeon. Bright herrings know nothing of their posthumous existence here rolled up in glazed shallow bowls of immense circumference.

Words at the head of my dictionary. I look for a spelling. I am intrigued on the way, and have found out the pomeloe, which is "a variety of the shaddock"; and just before that the polatouche, which is "a Siberian flying squirrel."

On my way I know a Paradise. In this Paradise there are no primeval parents, and no formal hunters. Above it the sky is poured coolly into position from five pallid towers of suavely insubstantial concrete. Intersecting railway lines enclose a triangle: this is my inaccessible Paradise. It contains rank shrubs, long grasses; and beasts which are not hunted, and protestant old Cranach painting them. And me, over Cranach's shoulder watching them.

Ahasuerus is to be observed climbing mountains: the lower ramps incline gently from Charing Cross Road and St. James's Square and the Yard at Harvard. Ahasuerus climbs slowly, he sees no one but a reflection of himself, he sees occasionally a Glory around the shadow of his head on mist below him. He has read Coleridge. He looks up to the next hold for his pudgy hand. He climbs, yet vertigo and the chance of falling are his pleasures. He has cut his beard short, vertical sunshine blisters his neck below his ginger hair. He has climbed out of sight.

On my way, the pathos of a literary party. I wait for my companion, to go up in the wheezy lift. In New York it might be a pert lift. I wait and I observe The First Cabinet of Mr. Gladstone. The party is promoted by a newspaper. The elderly recognize each other and talk of when they were young. The young are timid. The literary editor hands a cheque equivalent to the salary earned in a month by a police inspector or by a whore in a week to a she novelist who has written the five millionth novel since the first novel was written in English. What he says, what she says, nobody hears. What she has written, few at the party will read. The elderly talk of when they were young, the young are timid. Most in the room do not know each other's identity; or their own.

The pathos of a literary party. It is given, by his publisher, to honour the poet in the corner; standing in his coffin in the corner, protruding his head into the noisy room. This cadaver protrudes further into the noise a strong jaw, pitted and green. The jaw moves, but if this cadaver speaks I hear nothing. Are his poems good? Are we privileged? Is this an occasion which will be recorded in memoirs, or a journal? Did you write that review of my father's poems? Has this corpse a son who will be a publisher and will ask such a surly question in Boston, or Chicago?

Once, before all such were sent under cover, it was possible to see in every doorway along Brewer Street the blond aureoles of prostitutes shining in evening sunlight. It was as if angels by an early master stood in sunshine in diminishing perspective along a forest avenue in Savernake, obscene mushrooms pure among the leaves.

The acids of naming and of time which loosen structure and currupt the surface, permit the grasp of the affections. They do not attack these blocks of offices, number by number, which are blocks and do not rise to a tower looped by the unlikely rosiness of the morning or the more orange and comforting red of the evening. A tight arse (which did emerge from a womb) superintends the transfer of money in bags from hands I saw briefly in the opening of a security car, as if they were the hands of a Lazarus who declined to rise. A drawer in the basement is full of the dried skins of the polatouche, which is "the flying squirrel of Siberia", and this drawer is labelled in Cyrillic characters.

Here I note on my way eidetic visions in colours stood up in front of a poet. And here the nature of the incidence of cholera was observed from the loose dead, who had drawn from a single pump.

Along all of the squalid street under breaking buildings green avocadoes glitter in boxes. Polished fruits of bald heads of old salesmen, brown coconut heads of the

41

whiskered. Fog at the cross-streets changes from red to green.

HIGHGATE CEMETERY, LOOKING FOR THE GRAVES OF GEORGE ELIOT, MARX, AND SOCRATES, AND FOR WOMBWELL'S LION

To come here looking for the grave of Is
who obstinately is and always is I think
would not be wise.

To come looking for the grave of Was
I think as well would be
unwise.

Above a set of skull and ribs the presently
indicative inscription says—if not
'here is'—'here lies.'

Though I object, if you object that 'Is
and Was, God damn their eyes,
identically are lies.'

WHEN FINALLY

What shall we Stoics do
When, finally, we're faced
   With going under?

Pressing on the rounded
Flap of each ear won't
   Suppress that thunder.

A call on God—at last—
Will not at all
   Fight off our panic,

When the rafts have left
Us on the high impossible hills of
   Our *Titanic*.

O.K., O.K.,
Again repeats our motions,
   By long habit;

Myxamatosed, each man
Of us into a bulge-
Eyed rabbit.

* * *

Bombs fell, the pale
Citizenry ran and lied how
They could take it;

Like whom, the most we
Most of us can do
Is fake it.

EXPULSION

Driving them out,
Flapping from flowering tree to tree,
He manages his great blade's vicious
Fire as well as he can.

He was no good
Angel who did this to man.

AS DUFY PAINTS

Wise Coleridge says the happy poem is the best,
And English poets write of sadness best, or most.
There is, I do regret, our rhyming three
Sad, mad and bad: which do succeed the glad.
But, to be sure, as Raoul Dufy paints,
To write like the bright sap green
Which lights dry saddening banks
Beside charcoal of hard roads in the spring
(Adding rose madder and a deep sky blue)
For all of us is good; and is for the sadder
Writers, a most enviable thing.

A DAY MOTH AMONG JUNIPERS

Of that smooth
gliding moth I find
to-day the name;

Moth striped
as you'd expect it
not to be, I mean,

Long ways along
its wings with
black on white:

It was attended in
the sizzling sun by
dazzling Blues,

which
fluttered
commonly.

This other one,
this big one with black
stripes reduced

Its fluttering
to just
as little as need be

For height: was then
a smooth down glider
with wide wings.

You might say, that is
imagine, it disdained
that fuss

Above flat junipered
limestone under
white midday

Of, as you
might call them, its
attendant Blues:

But so descriptively
it is, or was, so
natures are,

And now I know,
which I need not
tell you,

Remembering its slow
glide or (from
the French)

Myself retain, this
not expected moth's not
necessary name.

THE WHITE DOVES

They rose out of dead men,
out of their mouths,
gently, white doves,
to branches where they fidgeted
at first a little,—
free, uncertainly.

It was something,
white doves for the souls of men,
instead of the roving idiots
of the morning, cuckoos,
or jackdaws cackling or identical
factory chickens chelping, or worse.

White doves
even the souls of the worst.

PICTURE OF A SATURNINE PROFILE

As if in a picture by an unknown master
I see a bald priest long-nosed, goat-faced,
Delineated over me in the unevennesses of the plaster.
He kneels, of course; his vestments encircle half his head.
I think he prays for the repose, which he thinks not
Likely to be granted, of an evil grandee at last dead;
Or he meditates on the stinking nature of man
Or of God rather by whose great guilt he supposes
Began our guilty and peculiar tribe of man.

My last half-hour in bed so invaded,
On a morning of late snow I write this down,
Look up, light has changed and my saturnine
Priest has faded.

THE CYPRIAN'S SPRING

The Cyprian's Spring by water only can be
reached, your pedalo moored to a hole in rock
on the slight slap of violet water. Press
your right shoulder to tearing rock along
a narrow path, brush the magenta
of wild gladioli, enter shadow, before which
also pomegranates flower. Swallows fly out,
the Cyprian's Spring breaks out, so many bright
gallons per cool minute, so many bright
gallons per cool hour, so many gallons
per cool century, so many glittering gallons
per cool aeon.
                 Swallows fly in, fly out,
in wild figs overhead are doves. Wet ferns
of black filaments slenderer
than the Cyprian's secret hair move
in the water breeze.

                Come here alone,
there is no room for two.

                Back in the arrogant
sun, if you upset your pedalo, and tumble
in, expect sharp stinging of purplish-black
sea-urchin spines.

THE GODS AND THE COLONELS

If one saw an actual snake
wreathing through an actual
skull's eye.

Instead I arrange such a tableau
with a rubber viper and a badger's skull
and have left it on the spare
room window sill.

And somewhere cold
clear water flows under
pink oleanders of
Theocritus—

whom I should, I think, now
spell Theokritos, de novo,
judge of the gods, accent
on the i—

without
cutting of the throat
of a white kid. But

the gods and the colonels
whom they serve, the whole
time insist
on blood.

TAME LIFE PARK

A duke, his bowlered daughter, a tenant,
    A scarlet-veined
   Arselicker, and a squire,
Look out expectantly on Saturday morning,
   From the wrong side of the wire.

On the Foxes, who spend their Saturday morning
    Poking lumps of sugar through the wire,
At a duke, his bowlered daughter, a tenant,
    A scarlet-veined
   Arselicker, and a squire.

WILD LIFE PARK

Flutters the fuckgale, standgale,
Galefucker (yes, names for him respectable
Dictionaries actually enshrine)—kestrel, windhover, kingdom
Of daylight's dauphin in his a little-dappled-flattened
Clinging to meshes of fine wire.

Trails from his left claw a chick: more such
Pus-yellow fluffs or powder-puffs of dead
Chicks from a farm
Sag under these wire-in naked branches dropped
By these half-dozen tedium's dauphins on this
Wet staleness of their ground.

A stink of fox, from curled foxes
Asleep on quarry ledges in the next cage,
Sneaks round.

Bristol, March II

55

SEQUENCE IN EAST CORNWALL

i Lansallos

Wet liverwort, wet rock.

Thread of a fall, and
spray;
joggling on stones until
the kettle's filled.

Mint is trodden. Wild madder
clings. Bartsia above, stiff,
shaking, the wind there brisk.

Then the small
stranded whale at an angle
just alive,
on the shelving beach,
its wide flukes convulsing.

ii Talland Sands

Fennel, smelt off your fingers:
is the tide out?
Then the Japanese bridge,
gap in the hedge, and red
bars of rock.

I kiss you, a flush
comes up your neck as red
as these smooth rocks.

I lose my nerve, and clothes
of others lie on the red rocks:
so we move on to
liquid ghosts of shrimps
in shallower pools.

iii   Off Polperro

It is the sun rising—I do not recognize it and I am
ribbed about it—out of the heavy
channel under which,
under us, under our stinking smack,
spreads the toponymy of rocks,
invisible, named rocks, named
ledges, hollows, named in extinct
Cornish, visited by the drowned
only, all the same familiar as
potato plots cut among matted
bent blackthorn along cliffs, to
fishers, out of Peter's porth or pool.

For centuries known;
at any rate before
they drank at fishing dawn
black thick sweet tea
from chipped enamelled rusted mugs.

iv   Longcoombe

Three steps in rock

under an ivied
oak leaning outwards
holding
in an old stick nest
dirty round
eggs of an owl.

But to you I attend,
not to the owl's eggs or
to whatever
home or mill has left
these bereft
worn steps

in wood-saged rock.

v   West Looe River

My darling, half-
naked among noisy flaked
leaves of cinnamon
off pearled beeches
high over a curl of the high
tide river.

Earlier it was among
bluebells, broken.

vi   Trelawne Mill

On the white plaster of the ruined cottage
you draw in two colours a goddess.
Now is it night. You have woken, by
candlelight in which you gleam,
you hunt hopping fleas
over the taut sheet, with a dampened
thin end of soap.

Hosh whimpers, wrinkled, in a dream.

It is day nearly. I have no doubt
of shining peal slipping
through the pools, upstream.

vii   Coldrennick

Upstream: rare osmundas, mundic,
the silver ore. Downstream a bog myrtle
thicket. In between, wet
moss-dome of a dipper's
nest below the bridge from which we
lean, we see foreshortened
the anyhow short
bird of white and black
move through the clear if
rippled stream.

Hold my cold hand.

viii   Botelet

Realization of emotions
as mimulus, yolks of eggs, lucid,
broken all along this stream:

so now I reject
the grey pampas plumes,
dry, snapped,

beyond the fastigiate
yews and the iron gate to our
cemetery, creaking.

Who lies there
is not you.

COTSWOLD COUNTRY

Her papa belonged to the Art Workers' Guild,
It was with Beauty he was filled,
In the Cotswolds he didn't care
If all the Jews were killed.

It comes of that: she pins the skull of a bat
Mounted in gold in her hat.
She hangs Concrete poems up in a mill,
And her breasts are flat, and it all comes of that.

FIGGINS

Who lived in Figgins Lane?
Figgins, shrewd toponomysts claim.

Which Figgins? It is fair to ask.
Committed to this formidable

Task, you advance your
Theory, you reply "Why,

Faithful Figgins. In the year
That pious man was mayor, his most

Unwary humped maid dropped
Her fourth miscarriage here."

Another Ph.D. says, No,
He can't agree: real

Figgins at this late
Date can't be found. Not

That I care. Figgins, I say.
It was some such

Coarse joke, I'd swear,
However long ago real

Figgins went to ground.
Figgins, I read in black

On white along
The corner plate, and I

Say Figgins, Figgins
For the sound.

CELEBRATION

Celebrate we the Great Nothing

Led by Coifi, Archpriest, in glorious vestment,
And by our long-nosed, horse-toothed
Archminister, in simple undress,
And by our Mayor in chain,
And by our Chief Lead Soldier,
And by our Head of the Humanist Association
Powdered with talcum,
And by our Poet of the Moment,
And by our white-haired Television
Star, masturbating, who is Renegue,
But calls himself Repentance,
And last by our Unknown Warrior,
In a new, but inexpensive suit,
Who is causing members of this distinguished
Company, as at the raising of Lazarus,
To pinch their nostrils.

Celebrate we the Great Nothing. But oh,
Celebrate we the Celebration.

Two minutes silence.

(N.B. The Royal Female Principle is away
Having her infertile womb scraped by the chief
Of her Royal College of Obstructions)

The guns boom.

There are no doves. Only absurd pelicans squawk,
Flapping their clipped and yellowed wings.

64

ABOUT THE ISLE OF MAN

(*For Archbishops and Cardinals, and
Headmasters at Prayers, and Brigadiers
at Church-parade, and the Queen*)

Since he began,
Man has thought—not surprisingly I'd say—
There's a Mystery about Man.
Who must be explained, and sustained, by a Plan,
By the G plan for Gods,
Or by the X plan for Odin up on a cross
Or Christ also aloft,
Or by the Y plan.
Particularly by the Y plan
(Or to judge by the favourite
fantasy-reading at present of Man it could be
he was made for a Spy plan).

I'm not sure it's the worse for Man
If for the first time since he began
He begins to realize there's been
No Plan for Man,
Who must now, Poor Man,
Do as they do on the Isle of Man,
Which is—What they can.

ANOTHER GREEN GRASSHOPPER

Drops of rain after night among crumpled pink
crossed by a green grasshopper.

No green as sharp occurs to me, not a green
wood on a map,
opened, reflecting pink rounded
clouds of foreign dawn.

The whole rose sways, and between two
triangles of green
muscle this green shape as still as can be
stays; but—if I bend to this
centre of scent,
from this pink centre of scent and
drops of rain—might
jump away.

This mineral crouches still, and
glinting drops have dried.
The whole rose sways.

Pink swing or carriage of this
most immobile green
grasshopper still in tinkling wind the
whole rose sways.

PEONIES

My poor peonies have by rain
Been in a circle beaten down,
Green tails together are birds lowering
Resonant and roseate ruffled crests
Along the wet garden ground:

Are brilliant yet.

THROUGH BUTTERFLIES

Not requiring to look into many faces,
    into yours only.
Not requiring to ask where that road goes.
    It goes.
I know its destination, I have no map only of
    its intervening track
Through dandelion grasses, then
    rippling of fords,
Climbing to a dry karst slowly; through
    butterflies, past
Debris of picnics, stones of the executed,
    and through junipers.

PLANE TREE IN A CHÂTEAU GARDEN

Every minute or so from the grand tree something descends.
Excrement of an insect tumbles, a leaf clatters, a scale
Of the grey bark drops off, revealing, if I could see, a yellow.
Also I watch leaves turn, leaves
Shiver, which hang at the end of branches which are not moved,
Which are zigzags high up.
                         I watch a white parachute
Seed of a minor plant: it floats, expedition
Of continuance losing hardly an inch of height
Through the space vaulted in a big way by these leaved,
Dividing zigzags. It crosses, and it floats
From view: I raise two hands and coldness
Of the stone bench in this great heat comes into me.

  Now I resent
Twinkles of sunlight which enter and interrupt,
And destroying voices, which come nearer.
My two hands raised, I know I should know this
Grand trunk, this grand branched vault impending.

Château de Poncé

WATER VOICE OF A DOVE

Resting in great heat by running water,
Yes, under a waving willow
By water we have called, viz. chuckling,
Prattling, chattering, I heard how a dove's
Voice is a voice of water, floating
On the voice of water, like the voice
Of passing water staying. So
I slept.

TO DIJON, UNDER SNOW

To-morrow I fly to Dijon, and to-day
Looking at the Master of Moulins'
Painting, at that baby in a Burgundy stable
Under his blue-dressed mother's
Thin astounded fingers,
Chancellor Roland kneeling, his fat dog
On his red robe, Burgundian shepherds
Watching from the green, I say,
As we say innumerably, *If*
This was so, If this was so,
If so ordinary a thing as a birth
Was so beyond all ordinary births,
If from the ordinary arose that extraordinariness
By which all was pardoned, all absolved,
Resolved. If just a little
Of this worked so—

And know that, holding us, a descendant, not
Discordant myth must grow.

THE COLD SPRING

Traveller, don't drink the sun-warmed water
Of this beck my trailing sheep have muddied so,
But climb the hill there where the heifers graze,
And go a few yards on, and you will find below
That shepherds' pine, bubbling from wet rock,
A spring colder than northern snow.

From the Greek of Leonidas

DREAM OF EXISTING

So I dream
once more that I visit one
of the out-islands of our archipelago
which rising higher than high cliffs are yet
secret with coombes cut into them
and with ladders of villages;

in which women
dress differently in a niche
of time, and speech
has microdialectical
differences; in which
I never get to the farthest
villages, fearing

always in my dream
I shall miss the returning
launch. I land,
off the great seas, the launch
quivering, climb streets resembling,
I say, ladders of stone,

of houses leaning across,
white, over
enormous hydrangeas and flowers
which are unfamiliar, blue lilies
in air watered,
tasting salt off my lips.

VIPER'S BUGLOSS

To cleared coppice I come,
scratched, on the hill
which savage bugloss all over
makes
a sea blue,
savage bugloss all over
makes
a sea blue.

AGAIN, BLUE

There is a most white black-centred
soft circle of snow around
a pot which stands on a square
of stone

half black half snow
and neighbouring stones
are so and from each
crack between

the stones half black half
snow round the exact soft
round of snow
between green stripes

of leaves a few grape-
hyacinths erect
erect
a blue.

THAT CONE OF A MOUNTAIN,
SUPERIOR,

known to Donne
in a ship where
musicians
played on the poop,

is most white
most white
up there, There—

Snow-Cat
of the air
high air

sleeps

on the high air
does not stir

sleeps
never lifts

its tail
from its ear.

White Cat
of the high air

ignorant
of spray down here
cut out of

sinking rising
of grey
down here,

of large-eyed
out-flipping

bright
fish from white
spray down here.

Up there, There—
quite still,
as light

lasts in the air,
sleeping, not conscious

Snow-Cat

most white
cat of the air.

NOTE ON THE UNTRADITIONAL

Lord, *My God*, *Your Temple*, his poems begin:
Differently others, including your humble,
Who are less avid of sin,
Repeat his ecstatic reverse of a grumble;

In which I consider he spoke
Of renewal of singing—it happens—by commonplace birds,
Of light down, golden section, hard structure, texture,
Sparkle, single and multiple curves.

These he left out, but I say his descendants
Have learnt it is far from a screaming sin
To leave out God and in grace
To put the facts in.

DESULTORY SUMMER POEM

i

It is a luxury, so circumstanced in summer,
Thinking of affection as abstraction,
Separate from you.

Clouds
Out of the huge cloud-gulf of the west
Come up, ferns of asparagus
Across them wave. One cloud
Passes, releases cool wind along my
Upper arm, then
Sting of the sharp sun.
A blue smoke rises from a yard below,
Thins to a less blue, and through
The mucked horizon of near trees a paling
Threads a close-set pattern down.

I scratch the bites across my wrist,
Hear leaves, observe blue smoke now
Against grey of a fat cloud re-
covering the sun; I think, I say,
Of this abstract of affection (you
Having gone to town) and, in
Some photo, of round Ionesco's
Face of a clown unbrutishly repeating
All's absurd.

My habits are not regular, I don't
Set periods aside or work by a clock.
I should do nothing oftener, think
Of you more and of affection
Less, eyeing always that
Which is automatic.

   I think, when she interrupted,
I should have given just now the slim
Gypsy child the two coins she
Held out her hand for. Some moments
Reveal too much and—just as well—
Are deliberately, quickly forgotten:
I was too lazy, I accepted
The estimate of gypsies,
Which may be correct; stopping the luxury
Of thinking of affection,
I should have gone indoors and fetched her
The money she asked for—Why not?
I acted
Like that balding Fool in London who's
Collected a Council of Fools to consider
Not their prurience but what they
Suppose obscene: the child followed
Her *métier*, I was stingy, I followed mine,
And it rains now and I am forced
Away from the sibilance of the sad bullfinches
In deep leaves behind me:
I should remember longer than I shall
That I was mean (not only because that
Child-gypsy was naked-footed
And was slim).

In the sky scene as I move I notice
The greyness of the underside of the great
Cloud now above me; and a round
Hole through this grey, and in this hole
Blue, and the white
Top of a thunder-cloud unseen otherwise away
In the queue of the clouds.
By this is excused nothing,
Illuminated nothing, symbolized
Nothing—unless accident, accident,
Can be described as something?
Such as myself or you? Such as the gypsy
Child, such as that noble ninny in London
(Whom I recall as a petulant
Blonde-haired undergraduate tossing
His wonder mop when he was found
Out in one more pious intellectual stupidity)?

   It is raining heavily. I shall
Continue, indoors, reading
Of the severer absurdity
Of the Archpriest Avvakum, adjuring
His Old Believers to stride into the flames
And fix themselves to the stake. "For this
We came out of our mother's womb. You
Will not be long burning. A twinkling
Of an eye, and the Soul is free."
The Soul.

   It strikes midday through the rain,
From the church above, for the second time.
I hear the burr of the car
With you returning.

A PAUSE ON HIGH DOWNS, IN A HIGH WIND, AFTER BUYING PIGNOTTI'S *GIORGIONE*

Angels, protrude your long thin trumpets glistening
Out far from your black shelf of cloud:
Greet, angels, with tender voluntaries of your perfection
The minute soul flying through vast freedom upwards,
Having left behind its sagged body in a shroud.

O if this could be so, I exclaim.
But to perfection
Have we imagined it. In such perfectness have
As well fresh trees against light, in light
Been painted. So much must be allowed.

APOTHEOSIS

On that small island—

    (When sea lies quiet, it's sea,
    Changing to plural when it rises)—
    Spume drove and stinging sand, and
    Pluralized high seas made it
    Impossible to reach mainland.

    That's how it was.

    Behind shelter of rock and rab
    Where my low tent strained, brewing
    My tea, having no thought at all
    About anything so ordinary or odd,
    I found me face to face with—well,
    What rhyme insists upon—
    With God.

What was God like?

    I suppose you have to ask,
    So I'll say
    He wasn't like the pocked clay mask
    Of Robert Lowell, or like
    The undertaker's wax of Lenin,
    Or like a splendid negro bronze
    From Benin.

    God had no splendour.
    God wasn't God the Father or de Gaulle,

God wasn't a dapper Thomist
From the Haute École.
God wasn't male, female or of inter-gender.
God was no noble bleeder.
Impossible to think God hissed at length
Inside the thighs of Leda;
Or ever learnt to whore well.
God wasn't Allah on a passing-out parade,
Or fresh, or lively, or even
Like a more decayed
George Orwell.

I couldn't say to this indefinition,
     Cleft for me, I couldn't offer him or it
     An aluminium mug of tea.
     The fact is in that spumed air
     God was dumb,
     Sat there and sucked his thumb
     (He had a sucker and a thumb),

     Then left as in-
     differently as he had come.

          I rowed across the strait
     As soon as the pluralized high seas
     Had dropped to one,
     In the serenest evening sun.

SHOP OF THE BOILED SWEETS

I breathe on the glass between
Me and the sweets, and they can't be seen.

If I go in for these sweets,
Shall I find a Greek harpy there,
Who laps the counter with red teats?

Or shall I find no Greek harpy there,
No counter, no boiled sweets, no ceiling,
Worse still no floor, nothing, simply
Nothing, inside this door?

PIGEONS IN KALE

From cover of a stony stream-tunnel of a lane
I see them on the extremely steep
Curve of a kale field
Outside in the sun.

I need no aid to see their claws are red, in glass
Circles glint their eyes, their fluffed smooth
Necks are an easy shift
Of mineral colours in the sun.

THE LAWN OF TREES AND ROCKS

It was on the flat of a valley, where for some cause trees stood back—
Trees had not been shuddered then by the heavy flint or the heavy
    gabbro axe—
Sunlight (between gold and diamond, hot and cool) illuminated
At a morning angle a most green sward,
Nearly bisected, narrowly, by a stream. This rippled, but never hid
The pieces of red quartz which were its descending slightly
    winding bed.

It was here they grazed, their movement provoked a scent
Of mint. The barbarian hominid concealed in leaves could
Not detect their hooves, but heard the tearing of their
Plentiful food: bull, cows, heifers, calves, Bos primigenius
Who would be painted inside caves, grazed
In this medium sun, and flicked a tail, moved,
And only seldom raised a head.

HOMUNCULUS

Beastly you are, wonderful,
tough, vulnerable,
damp Admirable, just out
of your black cocoon.

Enfolding you, I wonder
what name to give
to a book about
the world you are in, the young

leaf which holds you.

FICTIONAL VIEW ON THE EQUATOR

Damp heat in God knows what tropical
Eyot of abandoned empire
Under the huge leaves, sagging, of an undeciduous tree
A narrow man with ulcers repellent, who is, who was,
He seldom recollects, a Ph.D.,
His fat woman using her black thumb for digging
Jiggers out of the brown bosom resting on her knee,
And that novelist, that fallen angel, G.Greene,
(See *Macbeth* IV, 3) watches from the sick leaves
Of another poisonous hairy-fruited tree.

It is a common language which this climate speaks
Translatable from such excess humidity—
Ay me, ay me, soe much I sigh to see—
Into dry temperate terms
Of living graciously.

WOODPECKERS

After the Great Frost of 32
Few green, yellow, scarlet
Woodpeckers any more
Sloped round.

I picked up one,
How small, pecked, under the landslide
On the numb snow covering,
Under trees even,
Nearly all the ground.

The noise they make,
Ringing, I much missed
Heard in mornings
In sloping transit between
Trees all around.

The odd thing, starlings
Imitate it still,
So I have found.

THIS CLIQUE OF ISLANDS

To be this clique of islands scattered,
seeming to float though fixed across this indentation of
our lake in the entirely new cool light of one more, still
noiseless, exquisite day:

In their relation of light and levelness
to contain them, doubled, cool, by light
intervalled, also overlapping silently: to be them
at this second, as if

Always. Now. A tinny bell, a single thin voice hollowly
crying an answer out over the water to an unheard
question intimate of this place. Slight creak of a boat, slap
if gently of oars.

A wind, shortly, will come down or come up
turning a corner ruffling this clear-edged
campanile and its six trees of death and all
of its other attendant leaves

Exact on the unmoving water, removing this scent
of water. Don't you as well give way yet, my darling,
to this morning, shifting your firmness from me to which
I lean coolly.

EXCLAMATION ON CHILDREN
OF AN OCTOBER

Ah, my darlings who have low sun in your hair,
without a purpose going down the verge early,
under few leaves—they are waving;
shadows thinner of trees—over bluish-grey
grass they are moving; how scarlet big
dahlias depending.

Ah, my long-shaded, my
halo-headed, in this warmed air
of ending, ah my gay darlings in now,
in a now of first-morning
seeming joyously holy, low yellowing, yellowing, glow in your hair.

ORB OF WALT WHITMAN

Master of the great solitary lines
And the great sense of the world,
Child of its long beaches, empty once, O
Glad you would be if you knew
That your orb and ours
Is, in space turning,
A beauty
Streaked in blue.

INCIDENT IN A LIFE

On a heath in Dorset
Car parked by the road.
They wanted it,
Have had it, and that's that.

And comically—laugh, go on—
His damp foreskin balloons
Lopsidedly,
Having been bitten
Before or after by a gnat.

A COMMENT ON BUTTERCUPS AND THE REPLY OF A DWARF WHO LIVES IN A HOLE BEHIND THE CONSERVATIVE CLUB

Hell to these accustomed English buttercups
Of this bowl of dressed salad stuff
In which we live,
And to these blunt
Horse Chestnuts

Heaving in as usual June
5,000,000 flowers by gardens, open,
To prove owners
Better heeled than some. I say: "Dwarf,
Cut me a new rune."

"Revealing—if it can be read,"
You from your hole sneer, "just what? except
The last invariability
(It's vanity, your flag of red)
Of being dead."

IF WEARING MY OLD GOAT'S SKIN

If wearing my old goat's skin down Reviewer's Lane
I cried the birth of a Byron or a Blake again,
Who would look out, or even hear,
Or give up buggering his bald Teddy-bear?

BLUEBOTTLE

I shall not kill that spiralling bluebottle
with my poisoned aerosol. His wings
cut a genuinely charming murmur of
all past good summers through the room,
again, and again. If this present
good summer was done with, and he walked out
from underneath my papers and on his feet went
slowly and fatly round,
he'd be unfortunate.

TO PROFESSOR DONALD DAVIE

On a new nag old Carl Sandbag of Chicago
Rides again over a Grey Mountain
Where mist only succeeds a mizzling rain,
Above the flatitudes of an everlasting plain.

THOUGHT ON FUDGE AND CRYSTAL

There are many ways of making fudge,
The cubic products are all much the same,
In litteris
Fudging is what fudgers do
And fudge is the generic name.

In which physics of the word
Crystal is to be preferred.

PLACARD UNVEILED TO THOSE ENTERING
A FINE NEW HOSPITAL

Friends, agreed:
Each will have individually
His fill of age.
And fear.

You are not rats, or should
Not be, yet have, with you,
With yours, again agreed, no doubt,
No doubt at all enough to bear.

Yet—to ROOMS G 59 TO 86 AND
WAITING—*waiting*—ROOMS G, E,
AND O, and oh, the weighted
Shuffling into here.

God, a poor reed God knows,
Help you and all
For whom comes *Now*,
If you and all don't care.

BURIAL IN SEPTEMBER

The old ones go to each other's funerals,
The old ones mourn themselves.
It is sometimes in perfection of the weather
In, as now, the ending summer
When shoe-darkening wetness of the grass of lawns,
And graveyards, does not dry or dull
Until about the tolling of the bell.
Not even the cleric thinks of heaven,
No one who's here has visions of a hell.
Glad that it's over, sons go off to their gravid
Wives or to their girls. And driving
Home slowly, in their expensive limousines,
The old ones mourn themselves.

SNOW WHITE

Roofs white, lawns flatly the same,
Over all heavily lowly grey,
Trees without leaves, on one side
Lined snow white, so black as hell,
And snow muffed conifers more black
Still.

A flat bell stops, a dog howls,
Over all this snow I say heavily lowly
Grey. I again lean, years have gone by,
On my half-door, watching without thought
—A car splashes—close of a winter, close
Of a day.